Akanksha G Mittal spent her growing-up years at Ashok Hall in Majkhali, Uttarakhand amidst the magnificent Kumaon hills. Ever since, she has nurtured a deep love for nature and poetry. A district-level champion in badminton doubles from Almora, she is equally drawn to theatre, fine [illegible] photography and horse-riding.

Akanksha, [illegible] from Jesus and Mary Col[illegible] en writing poetry, reading, [illegible] king after the Punjab chap[illegible] sibility of a leading conglo[illegible]

The Sound of Silence

Akanksha G Mittal

Om Books International

Sushant,

A dream dreamt of a dream,
and you were born, it seems.

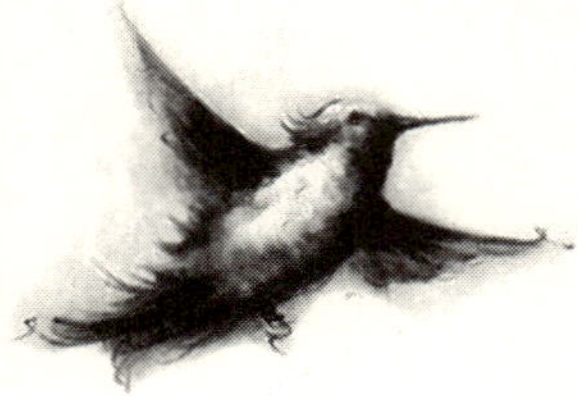

First published in 2018 by

Om Books International

Corporate & Editorial Office
A-12, Sector 64, Noida 201 301
Uttar Pradesh, India
Phone: +91 120 477 4100
Email: editorial@ombooks.com
Website: www.ombooksinternational.com

Sales Office
107, Ansari Road, Darya Ganj
New Delhi 110 002, India
Phone: +91 11 4000 9000
Fax: +91 11 2327 8091
Email: sales@ombooks.com
Website: www.ombooks.com

Design concept: Arijit Ganguly

ISBN: 9789352766369

Printed in India

10 9 8 7 6 5 4 3 2 1

Contents

Acknowledgements

I am deeply thankful to:

Both my mom and dad, for being my anchors, for guiding my every step, for teaching my heart to feel, and for your unconditional love and support for which I shall forever remain grateful;

My brother, Rahul, for always protecting me and spoiling me. I love you. You are my best friend;

My beautiful sisters, whom I look up to:

Swati for being my partner through thick and thin, and for being the one who listens and understands;

Sagrika di, for being my star, and for helping me put life into my words;

Geetika di, for gracing my life and looking after me with unparalleled support and guidance;

My amazing crazy friends, my circle of long-time support, for adding laughter at every step of my journey and for listening to my midnight rants. You know who you are;

My fluffy friend, Sir Alfred, thank you for choosing us, expanding our hearts and teaching us that love truly is endless;

And special thanks to my readers, for believing in me and picking up *The Sound of Silence*. Right now, you are holding my heart in your hands.

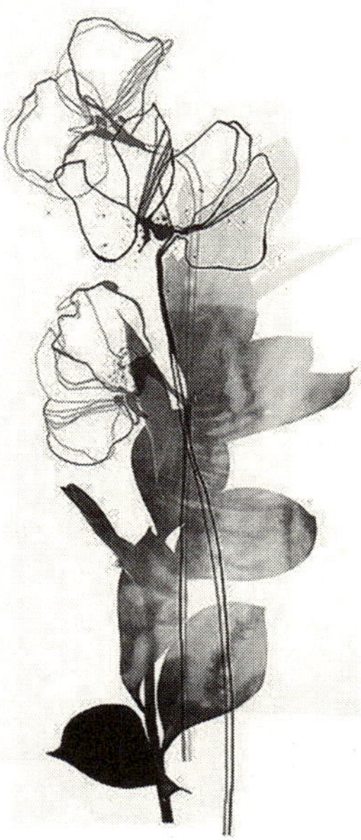

A blizzard

We are stuck in a blizzard of do's and don'ts,
Love petrifies us to our very bones.
But like flowers blossom at the first ray of light,
A bright day must always follow a dark night.
Even stars in the sky find their way to the ground,
Like seasons changing all year round,
Like the waves wandering off to the shore,
But only to return to the ocean for more,
I hope love too finds a way to you and me
No matter how far apart we are damned to be.

Sweet poison

He wasn't the one to talk much,
While I kept mindlessly going.
My heart snuck out into his arms,
Without my so much as knowing.

I'd wait for him to say something,
Only to have him utter nothing at all.
Not even a word to make my heart sing
But his eyes scribbled on my wall.

His unblinking eyes tried to read me,
I who was a sailor willingly lost at sea,
Yet quiet and still he chose to be,
As though in a kind of secret glee,

Even in his stony silence,
All the right words had he said,
And their cascade and cadence,
Foretold a sweet poison to dread.

Thoughts insane

How can I expect to fathom you,
When I can't my own thoughts insane?
One minute I see a rainbow, or is that two,
And the very next moment, it starts to rain.

Happiness in a bowl

When your heart feels too low
To even want to beat.
And you don't want to let go,
Burdened by words you cannot speak.
I'll tickle all your bones,
Serve happiness in a bowl,
Chase out all the groans
Put laughter back in your soul.

The lonely sky

The ground and sky parted,
So the world could form and life come through.
But often the lonely sky cries river,
The only way it can touch the ground,
I think it feels homesick too.

Hear me call

When the skies pour rain,
Like kisses of death,
When the world is insane
And we gasp for breath,
When peace just falters,
And the last leaves fall,
When your heartbeat alters,
Will you still hear me call?

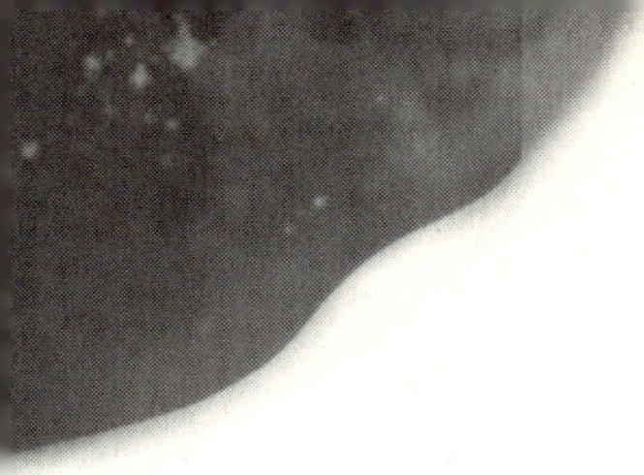

Envy

Let your love take me
To the top of the sky,
That even birds envy,
For they can't fly so high.

My shadow

I shed the person I used to be,
To change the way I used to see.
The world was then cast in a new hew,
As my smitten heart began to follow you.
Now my shadow resembles you,
My heart seems captivated too.
Yet I've never felt more free,
Despite forgetting all I used to be.
Today when everyone looks at me,
It's only you they can ever hope to see,
And why would I ever begrudge you that
When I don't recognise myself without your hat?

Butterflies

These butterflies won't settle,
Not tomorrow, not today,
Not even when the lone petal
Kisses the grass on a foggy sway.

Why trap them in a glass jar?
That's not how they're meant to be.
Creatures like them must fly afar,
That's what the heavens decree.

When behind us are years of clutter,
And many rebirths too,
Butterflies'll still set my heart aflutter,
At the very thought of you.

Tremors

One day I saw an enormous bright light,
And then the day slowly turned to night.
Suddenly everything just went numb,
But far, far away a light shone glum.
It was then for the first time I saw you,
Would you be mine? asked my heart so true.
At the snap of a finger, you disappeared into thin air,
Leaving stardust behind, and my existence bare.
Even your dust had shone like one of a kind,
Bringing me to my knees, in love so blind.
Into oblivion my heart seemed to sink,
Would you reappear if I were only to blink?

In worlds within worlds, I looked for you,
Searching high, low, through and through.
Raindrops wounded me, causing so much pain,
And the downpours hit me, again and again.
When the ground trembled, I just stood tall,
Praying the tremors would not make you fall.
Oh I looked for you dawn to dusk till dawn,
Till in disbelief I accepted that you were gone.
In the palm of your hand I can still feel my bones crush,

At night I drift to the places where you made me blush.
Though its day now, nothing shines as bright as you once did,
My feet don't follow my mind, no matter how firmly I bid.
My heart is in pieces, my soul is torn,
At the end of the road, my spirit is worn.
There once resided galaxies in me,
Now I am just all hollow and empty.
I'm not looking for you anymore, it's over, the tide,
So do come out now from wherever you chose to hide.

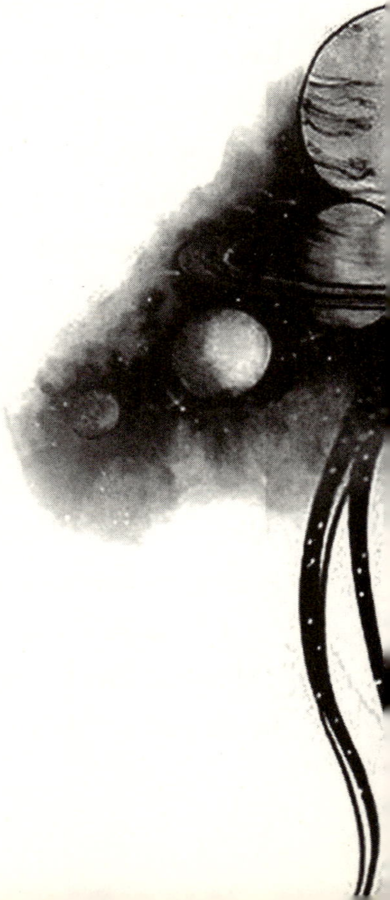

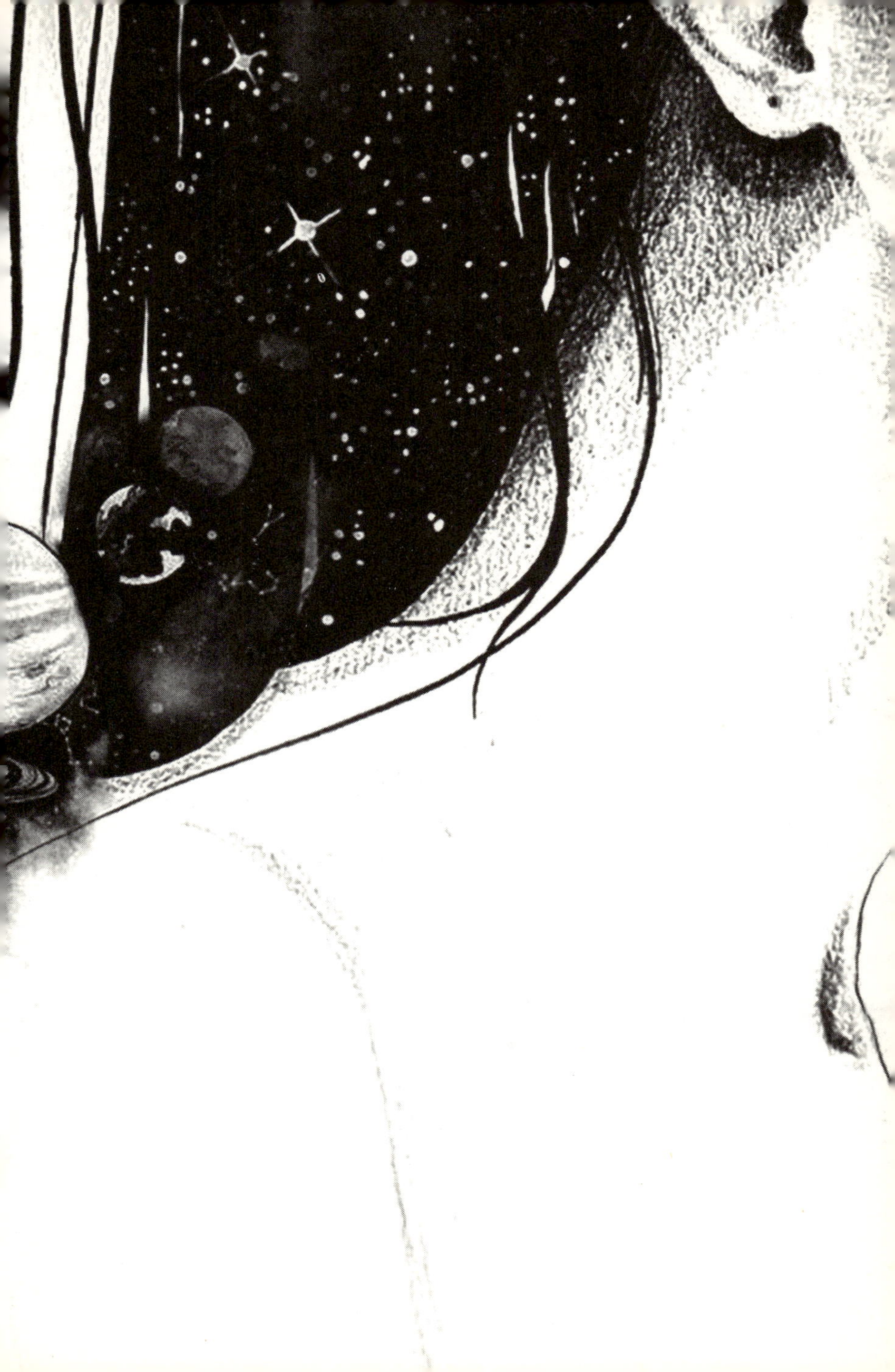

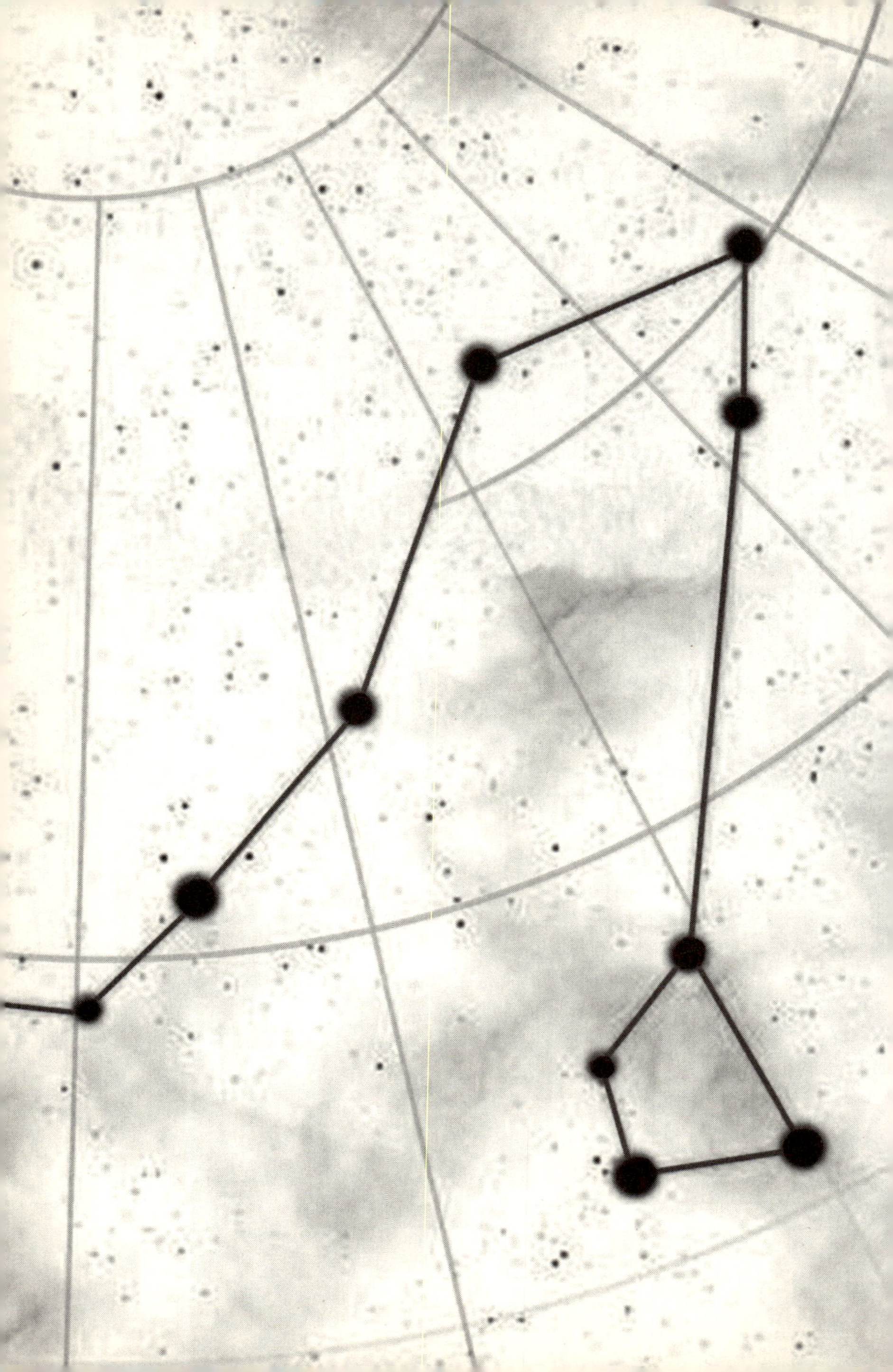

Volcano

He was like a volcano,
The thought made me want to jump in even more.
I knew I would burn down to ashes,
For his touch alone could create a thunderstorm.
He was deeper than the ocean,
The depths of him, so dark but so magical,
He beheld me in unmatched fascination,
His aura, where the stars formed constellations.
His silence was the deadliest violence I'd ever witnessed.
His smile, held the devil in him,
And it took me right to sweet hell.
He was everything I should've ran away from,
But I jumped right in.
And I'm what remains after the hurricane.
I knew this life wouldn't be enough,
Or this heart for all his eyes offered.
He poured some gasoline,
Burned down the hell in me.
He set the devil in me free,
From the moment I saw him,
I knew he would be the death of me.

My home

Our worlds might be different,
But your heart is still my home.

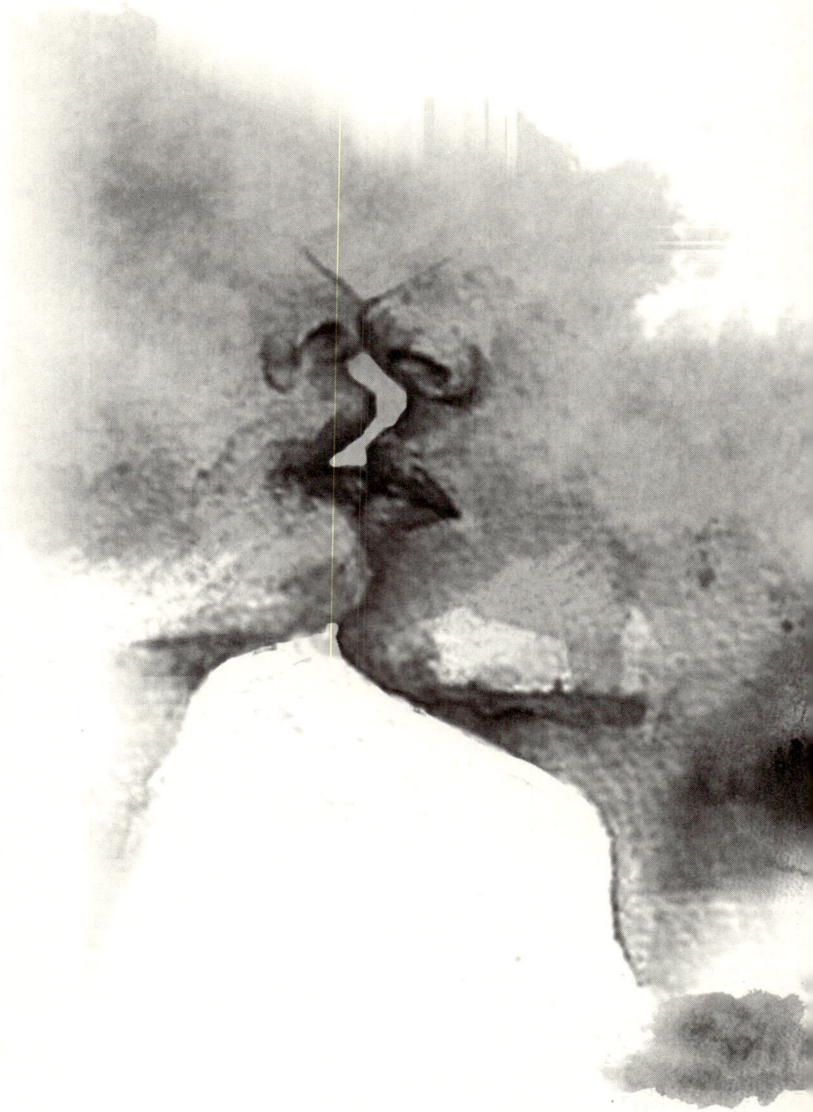

A symphony

The thing I want to learn from you,
Is to smile the way only you do.
The smile that warms my heart on a winter night,
The one thing that make all the wrongs right.
When you smile, it puts a smile on my face too,
Everyone may smile, but no one smiles quite like you.
When your lips stretch so wide and far,
Nothing beats that sight, not even a shooting star.
Like a song come alive without a word,
Your smile is a music no one has heard.
It holds my heart hostage, but sets my soul free.
What comes so naturally to you is a symphony for me.

His eyes

His eyes are miles of blue,
A combination of ocean and sky,
You could be drowning,
At the same time come alive,
That's the intensity in his eyes.

My bereft pen

Every passing day I wrote of you,
In a desperate bid to keep you alive.
It was the only way I could live too;
The only way I could survive.
But I was unprepared for what became of you,
Now you haunt me, and my bereft pen, too.

Why?

It'll tear through you,
You'll first feel numb.
It'll hurt like hell too,
And you'll just cry some.
You'll even ask God 'Why?',
Before your tears run dry.
Then again you'll go numb awhile,
Until you find another reason to smile,
Then laughter will follow and you'll shine,
All over again you'll see the stars align,
And you'll thank yourself for just trying,
That's when your tears'll truly start drying.
Keep trying when trying feels so wrong,
That's the only way you'll end up strong.

Wings

When my wings were set on fire,
And I was forced to fall to the ground;
I learnt that one needn't fly and inspire,
And suddenly I was truly sky bound.

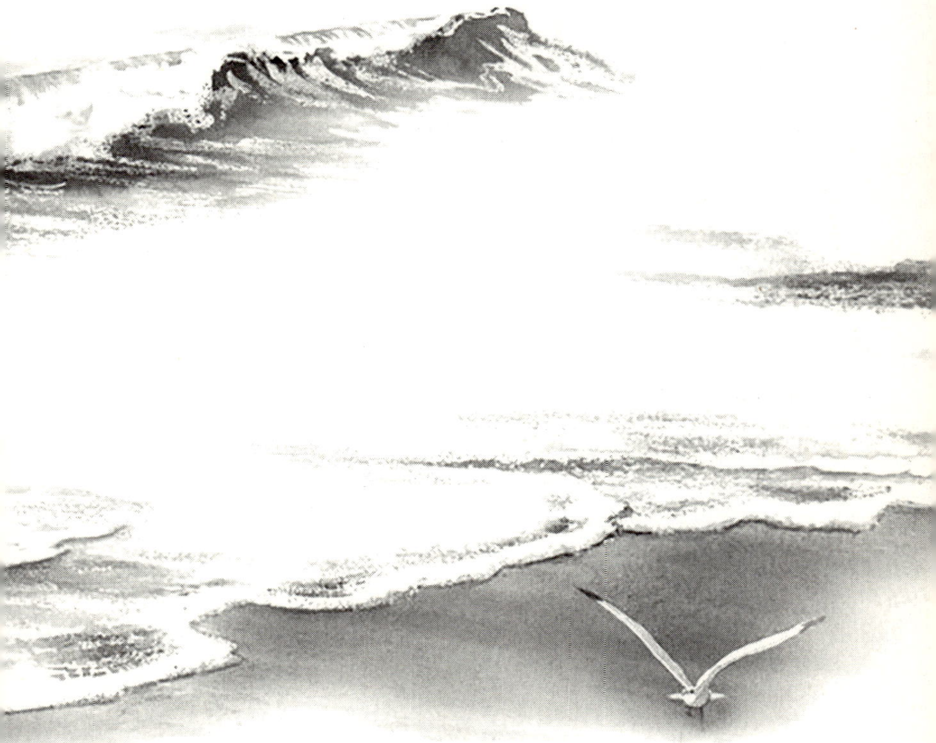

The magic

I dreamt everything went back to Adam and Eve,
Those were the two with their hearts on their sleeves.
There was a time with no words, just actions,
When we lived life whole, not just in fractions.
But then I saw the world of today,
And woke up feeling dismal and grey.
With a sinking feeling in my heart,
I saw people tearing people apart.
Oh, how I wish more and more people would believe,
That magic happens from wearing your heart on your sleeve.

Uphill

We seek each other out,
Without a shadow of doubt.
From far we reel each other back,
Let's not run anymore, it's time to unpack,
These crumbs of clues that we leave,
While with longing our hearts heave.
I just know you know what I mean,
The same need in your eyes I've seen.
It doesn't really matter where we are,
Those stars still beckon us from afar.
Things might change, but I know we never will,
From here, we can only go one way—uphill.
It's love on which your heart is set,
That's what you know but don't know yet.

I met you

I once created a world in my head,
A collection of every fairytale I'd read,
I lived in an ocean of fantasy,
Unwilling to settle for another reality
I feared no love would ever do,
Until I met you.

The brink

Each time the wind whispers your name,
My heart begins to sink;
Like the autumn leaf crumbling to pieces,
I teeter on the brink.

I slowly drift

Sing the song of the stars to me,
Make the galaxy sway as we.
Hold my hand and spin me around,
Nothing stands between us, neither sky nor ground,
The moon will hum our song as it shines,
As I became yours, and you become mine.
I look at you and smile the only way I know,
Stay with me; live in the moment, don't let go.
And as you hold me close to you,
Making me fall in love, like you always do,
I stay enchanted by you and your charms,
As I slowly drift off to sleep in your arms.

My heady desire

Like water and a wild flame,
You soothed my soul, then set me on fire,
As the flames torched my heady desire.

In minutes, my entire frame,
Lay reduced to ashes on the ground,
Yet I heard my faint heart pound.

Alas, I had verily burnt down,
Flesh to bone, name to pronoun,
But the sun on fire had to swoon,
And find a lover in the calm moon.

So while I was set on fire by you,
You set about dousing the flames too.

Rainbows

Thank you for creating rainbows,
When all I saw was rain.

An unparalleled dream

All my words become you,
How beautifully they come alive.
All we just really need to do,
Is make our beautiful love thrive.
You are an unparalleled dream
Passionate and wild as a lover.
But you're also that extreme,
That makes me stay yet run for cover.

And as I scribble about you,
My words seem to become art,
And to believe that that's so true
Gently lay your hand on my heart.

Story

Your eyes are my continuing story,
From a life before this one.

A love like ours

’Twas dark without a star in sight,
Thick clouds possessed the sky.
The heady heat overpowered the night,
Did we really need to guess why?
Were the stars not to witness our desire?
Was the sky meant to shy away?
As we both were ravaged by the same fire,
Till we collapsed with a heave and sway?
Turn away dear sky all you must,
For, though you do love the stars,
From ashes to ashes, dust to dust
You’ve never seen a love like ours.

Rhythms

These rhythms you'd set my heart in,
Their beats I could feel all over me,
As if they'd broken loose in a silent din,
Till I let myself be pulled out to sea.
You were a man so out of his time,
Impish, serene, yet utterly sublime.
I knew I simply didn't stand a chance,
All it took was a long piercing glance.
Out of my depth I hopelessly became,
And all that my soul could guarantee,
Was I would never again be the same
Or return to where I'd set out as me.

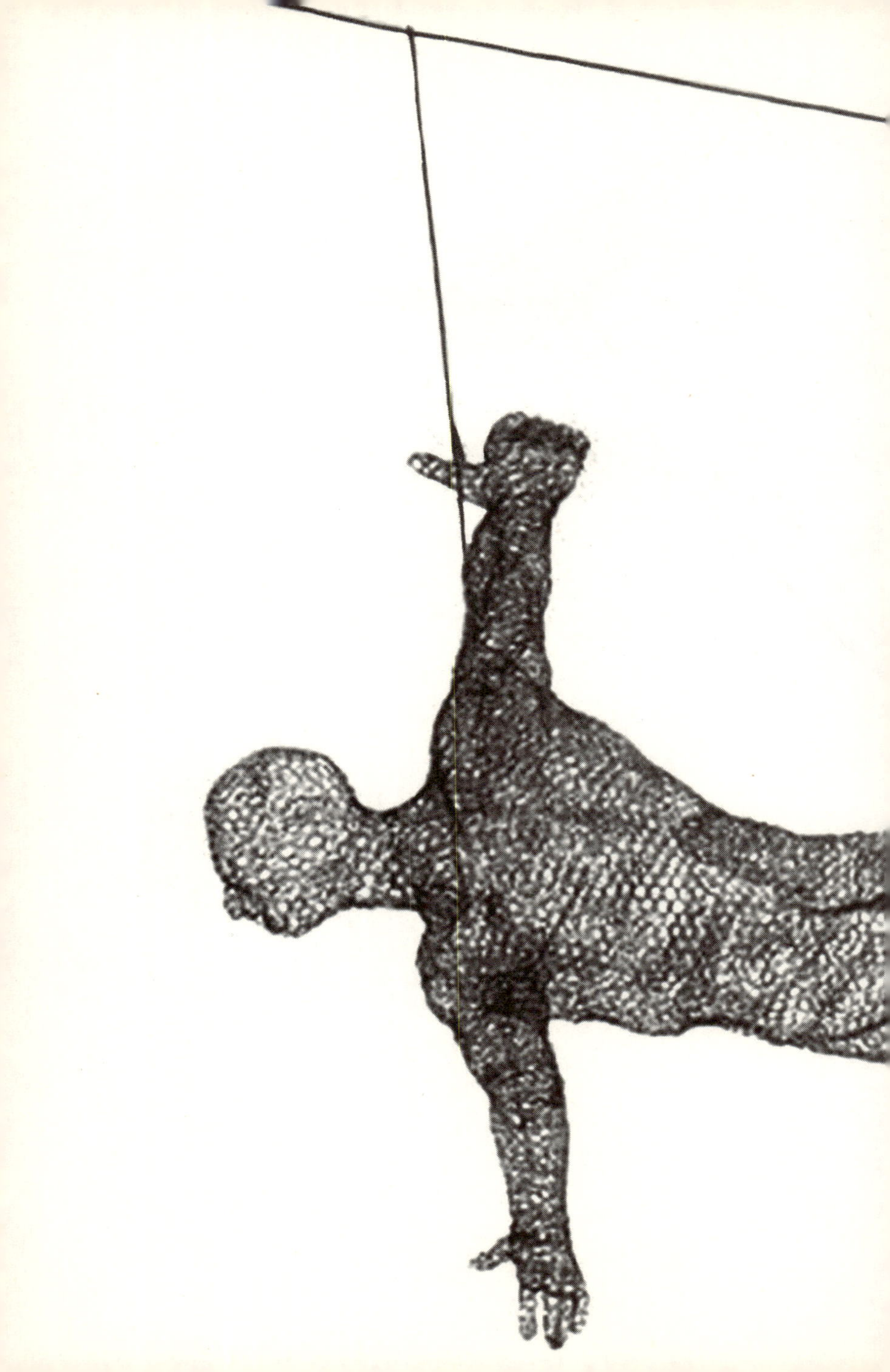

Insane

We grow up,
Hoping and praying to be kids again,
But the ones who managed to stay the same,
We call them insane.

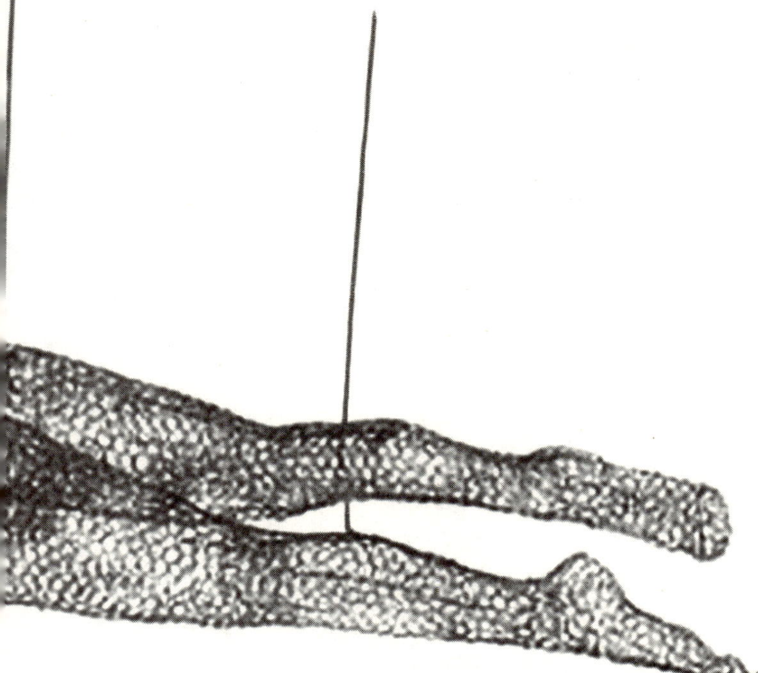

No tomorrow

If love were fire,
We'd burn in these flames forever.
Soaked in desire,
Emerge from this pyre, we'd never.

If love were an ocean,
We'd surely drown to its depths too,
Without any notion,
Of just how to unglue me from you.

If love is magic,
I'm hopelessly enchanted by you,
And its sweet music
Makes me want to live life anew.

If love were dismay,
We'd be doomed to live in sorrow,
If love were only today,
There just would be no tomorrow.

A little bit of me

I left a little bit of me in every book I read,
In every person I met, in every place I'd tread.
In every dream I dreamt, I left a little bit of me,
Till there was hardly even a cell of me left to see,
And then I became the person, I was destined to be.
Without baggage or burden, completely bereft of me.

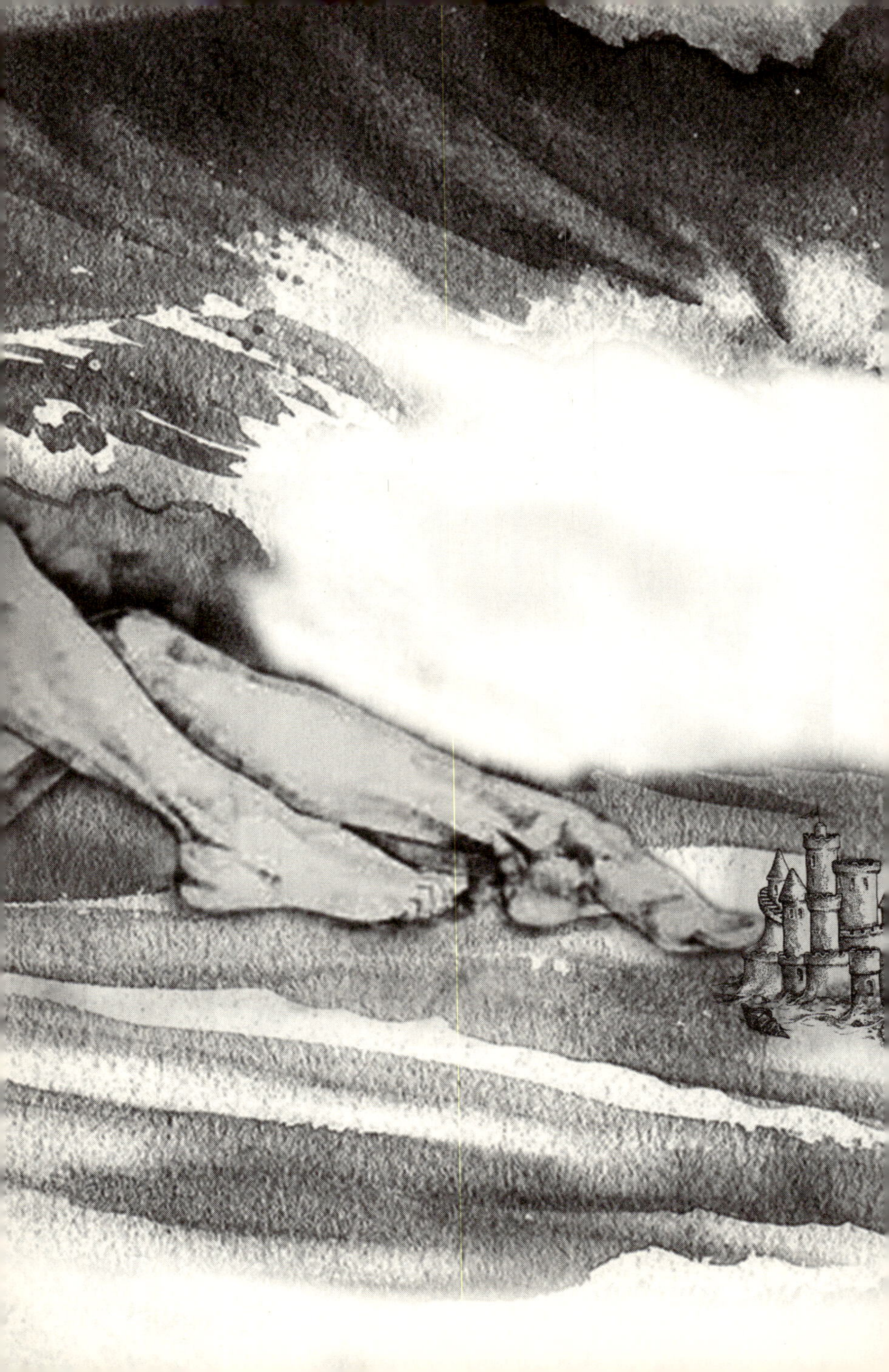

A sandcastle

A sandcastle I sure was,
Hopelessly in love with the wave,
But the end was worth it,
For I had the entire ocean as my grave.

Fire

When you touched,
My body froze like ice,
But my soul was set on fire.

Talking about thee

My heart has skipped an emotional drought,
I love you without a shadow of a doubt,
So much so, whenever I'm asked about me,
I seem to always end up talking about thee.

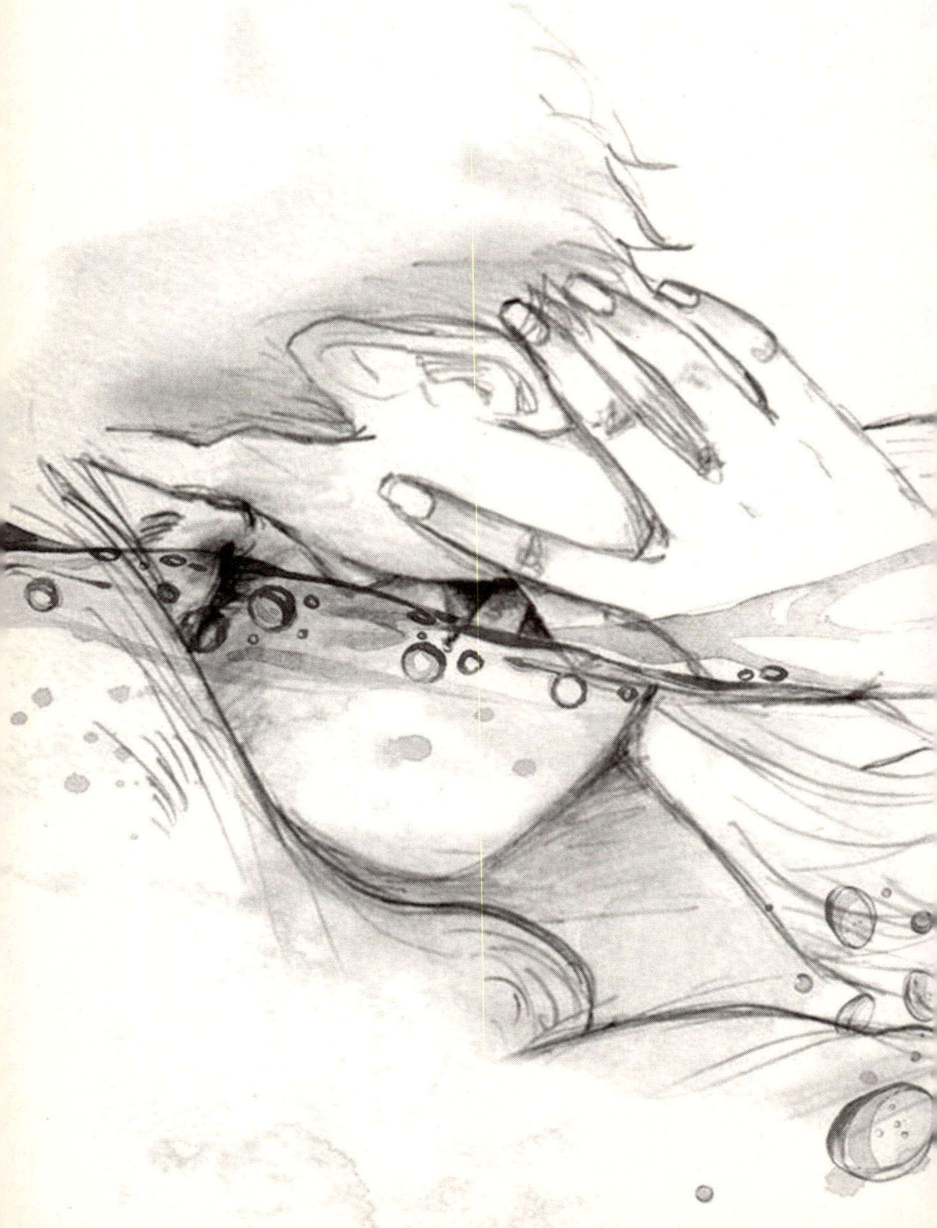

My share of air

If I were slowly drowning
Into the depths of the sea,
Without time for clowning,
Would you try and save me?
For if I only had,
But one last breath to spare,
I'd only be too glad,
To give you my share of air.

The beginning of me

I have been in you,
Since the beginning of me,
Like heartbeats are to the heart,
You are music to me.

Crafted

Like God had to create the sky after crafting the ground,
Once He had crafted the lips, He had to invent sound.
And when He formed the clouds, He had to make rain too,
I too had to be crafted because He had already created you.

The ground and the sky

The ground fell in love with the sky
The entire world just wondered why.
Rumours spread that they somewhere meet,
That both look forward to such a treat.
But no matter how the ground and sky tried,
On not uniting with each other, they cried.
Disappointed and hopeless, the sky went blue,
The ground burned with its desperate fire too.
Destined to love but never to meet,
Their pain was more than bittersweet.
What could they do when fate had conspired,
To make them wander alone till worn and tired.
Suddenly the sky cried to ease the ground's pain,
After a long stretch, the ground felt joyful again.
Now they live forever in each other's hearts,
While the world sees them as forever apart.

Gravity

If it weren't for gravity,
I'd fly to you tonight.

My poetry in you

Not that I didn't love poetry before,
Just fell short of words and their lore.
All I knew was that the sky was blue,
That the vast oceans reflected that too.
Then one spring day, I met you,
In the blue sky was something new.
The world was no longer the same,
I wanted to play every little game.
And then I knew that words meant more
Than scribbles on a paper or a mere chore.
It really was then that I knew,
I'd finally found my poetry in you.

Sleep

Your touch heals my soul,
That's why I hug you when I sleep.

Who's who

Addicted to love are you, I hear
I wish I were a drug too, my dear.
We could just lose ourselves in each other,
For days, nights, without a care or bother.
Love me till we can no longer remember who's who,
And again till we no longer recall we were once two.

love

Aeons before

Even before there was any alphabet,
And aeons before we could have ever met,
Your name was imprinted on my soul,
For making my half-self a complete whole.

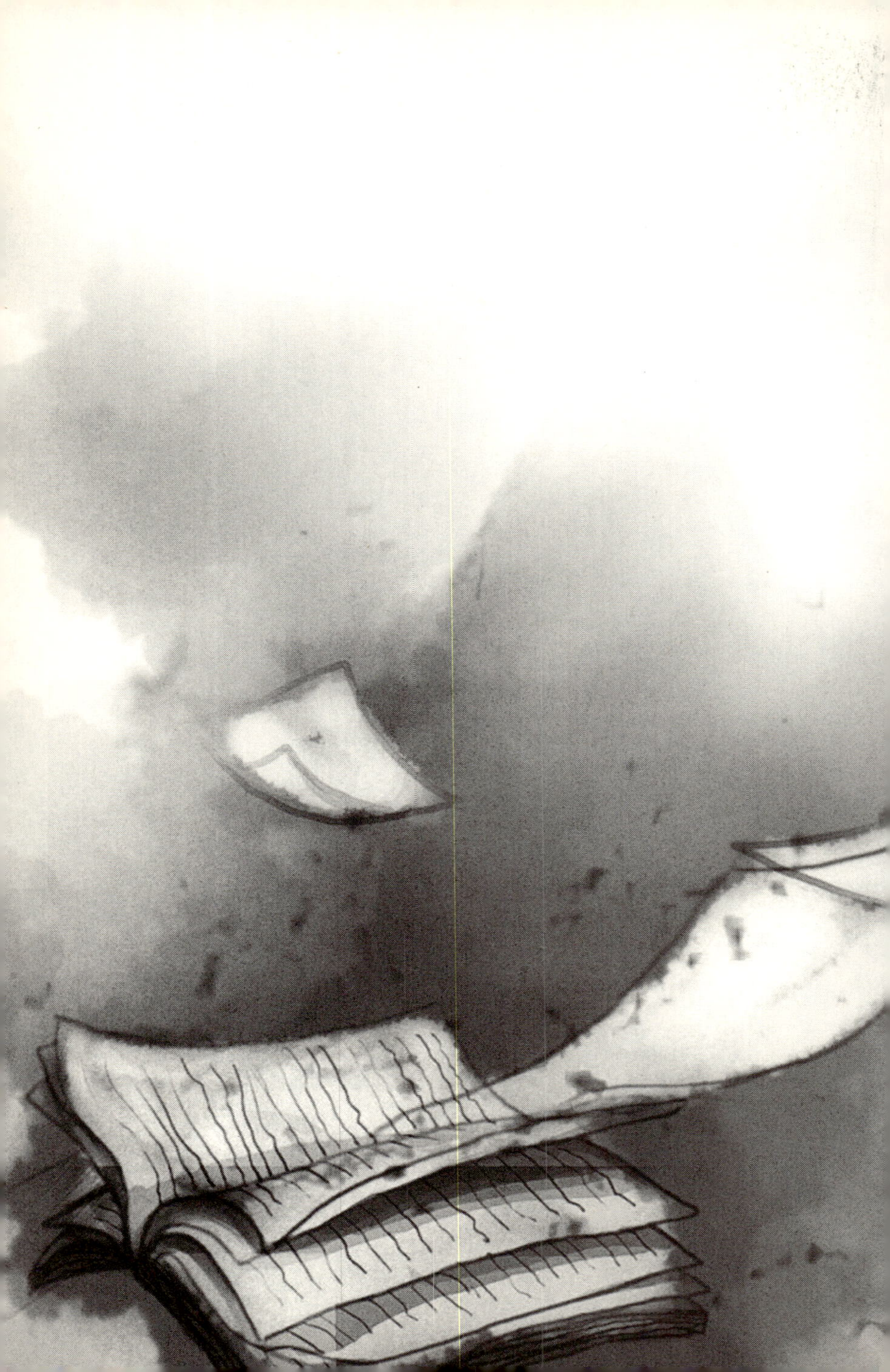

The way you breathe

It's easy to be a poet around you,
Even on your worst days,
There's poetry in the way you breathe.

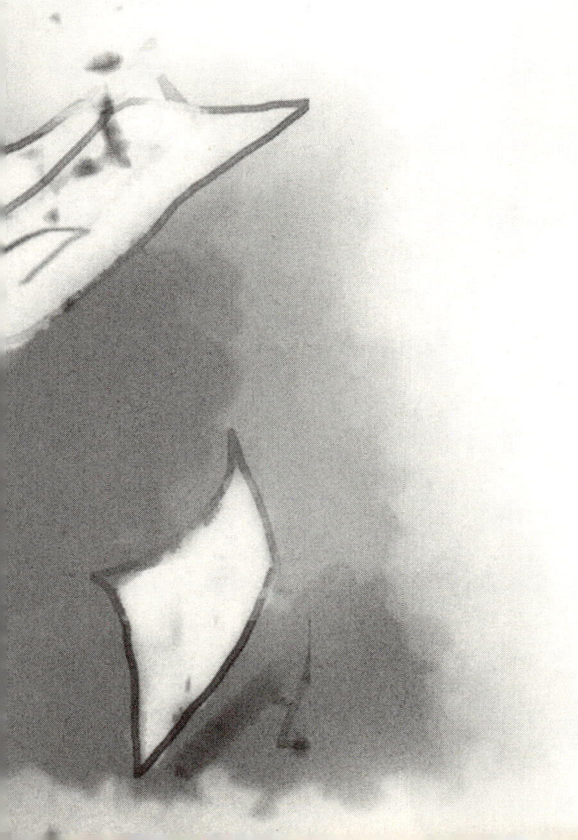

In the end

Why must I believe we are made of stardust,
And in the end that's what we'll turn back into?
And while in the Lord Almighty, I repose my trust,
I have reason to believe that I'm made only of you.

A tiny cloud

When the ocean comes alive,
How does the ground survive?
What if the birds never stop to fly,
And I paint another colour of the sky?
Why can't time stand still when those moments matter?
At your touch why must my heart race, my being scatter?
How do those moments just make me fly so high?
And why must they suddenly end? Why, O why?
Shall we really turn into stars when we die?
Shall love fade one day, no matter how hard we try?
How would it feel to hold a tiny cloud in my hand?
If the earth is round, shall the sky ever meet the land?

The twilight sky

As the twilight sky slowly gives in,
To the dulcet tones of the golden bright moon,
As the dazzling stars take over the sky,
Leaving the world spellbound too,
I stay enchanted and mesmerised too,
But by you.

Broken pieces

Perhaps one day we shall meet,
If not in body, at least in soul,
As our million broken pieces come together,
In an impossible bid to make us one whole.

I was home

When we hugged,
I didn't break into a million pieces.
My heart didn't sink or sigh.
I felt the most whole that I could.
The way your hands wrapped around me,
They seemed to have a hold,
Even my skin didn't have on my bones.
It felt like my soul was knocking on the door,
And when you hugged me just a little tighter,
I knew I was home.

Dreams

Why must I always be so wary?
Why is falling in love so scary?
Little do I know what's in store for me.
Will I make it through? I have to see.
But what if I just fall on my face?
Will you pick me up with gentle grace?
But isn't falling asleep scary too,
Till those dreams come looking for you?

Shades of blue

All the things that make you strong,
Come only once life has broken you,
Like the sky with colours, right or wrong,
Shall be known for its shades of blue.

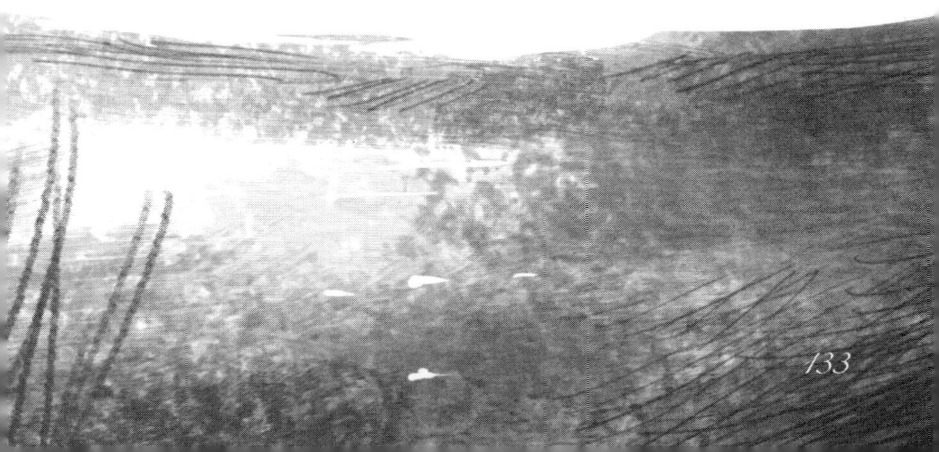

A farther path

I'm tired of seeing the same people, the same faces,
So full in their heads, and so empty in their spaces.
Please take me away from here, to a land far, far away,
And if exists a farther path, please take only that way.

Mosaic

Broken pieces create mosaic,
And you are oblivious to what you can become.

Our Paris

We merely live out our today,
Dreaming of a distant day,
Despite the taste of love's whiskey and rum,
When smoke in the sky all shall become.
Only towards love we should be inclined,
Leaving every other feeling far behind.
Only then shall we begin to see clearly,
How much we love each other dearly.
We'll finally connect every little dot,
That makes us all a part of our lot.
And we'll realise how everything magically led to this,
And behold for ourselves how beautiful everything is.
On that day, we'll find our Paris evermore,
Like a city of love never experienced before.

Heaven's gate

You want to know how to survive?
Just be the part, and be alive.
Put on a smile for a while,
Leave behind all the guile.
Bring some sparkle in your eyes.
Forgive people all their lies.
Wish everyone the very best,
Kindness, that's your final test.
Try and keep everyone's trust,
That just surely is a must.
Soft in your heart, strong on the crust.
In life keep your faith and your trust.
What did the elders mean when they said,
'If in God you believe, you'll keep a sane head?'
I'm not saying that the entire world is hollow,
But in your weaker times, it's you it'll swallow.
You were born as only you,
So to yourself you must stay true.
And when you reach Heaven's gate,
Because of all the magic in your fate,
Tell God, you did what you could,
That amidst all evil, you remained good.

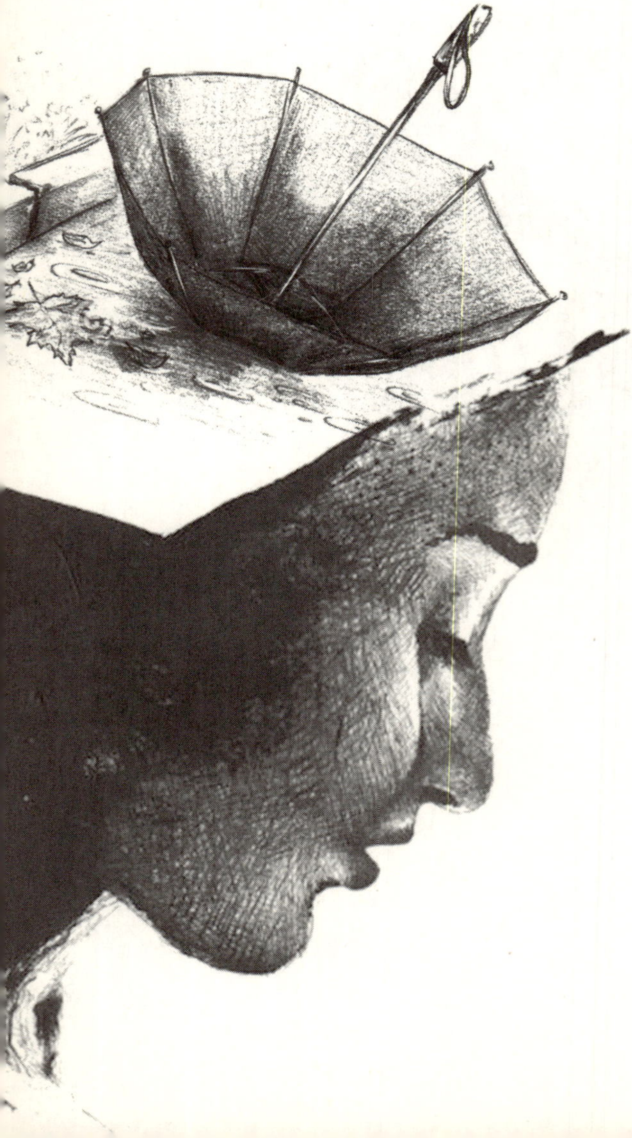

His smile

Loving him is effortless.
Even on rainy days,
There are rainbows in his smile.

A bit like me

You became the missing part in me,
You became the vision, so I could see.
You became my only key,
You unlocked me completely.
You became my everything,
And to you, I lovingly cling.
You gave me wings to fly,
No longer do I need to sigh.
You became the air I breathe, the magic and the miracle,
Making me drown in your love so true and so lyrical.
When you came by, I'd failed to see,
That one fine day you'd set me free.
And now I look upon you with glee,
As you too have become a bit like me.

Stars

He craved to hold her,
Like the galaxies hold the stars.

An aching heart

Tell me, my love, where have you gone?
You were the only light that on my life shone.
Wherever you are, does it feel like home?
Is it someplace where you can run or roam?
Are you somewhere cosy and warm?
Safe from thunder, hale or storm?
Do you have a place to mess around,
And leave your dirt marks on the ground?
When I couldn't love myself, you loved me,
How could you just so unconditional be?
Its so quiet now that you are gone,
To another world, you've passed on.
Gloom has possessed my lonely nights,
As I remember all our playful fights.
How can reality cause so much pain?
Why did you leave? Who was to gain?
Breathe for me, just once more please,
Put my distressed soul at some ease.
If you get lonely, think of me,
By your side, I shall always be.
Angels celebrate, for they have you,
What's left now for me to do?
And even though today we're so far apart,
You've never been closer to my aching heart.

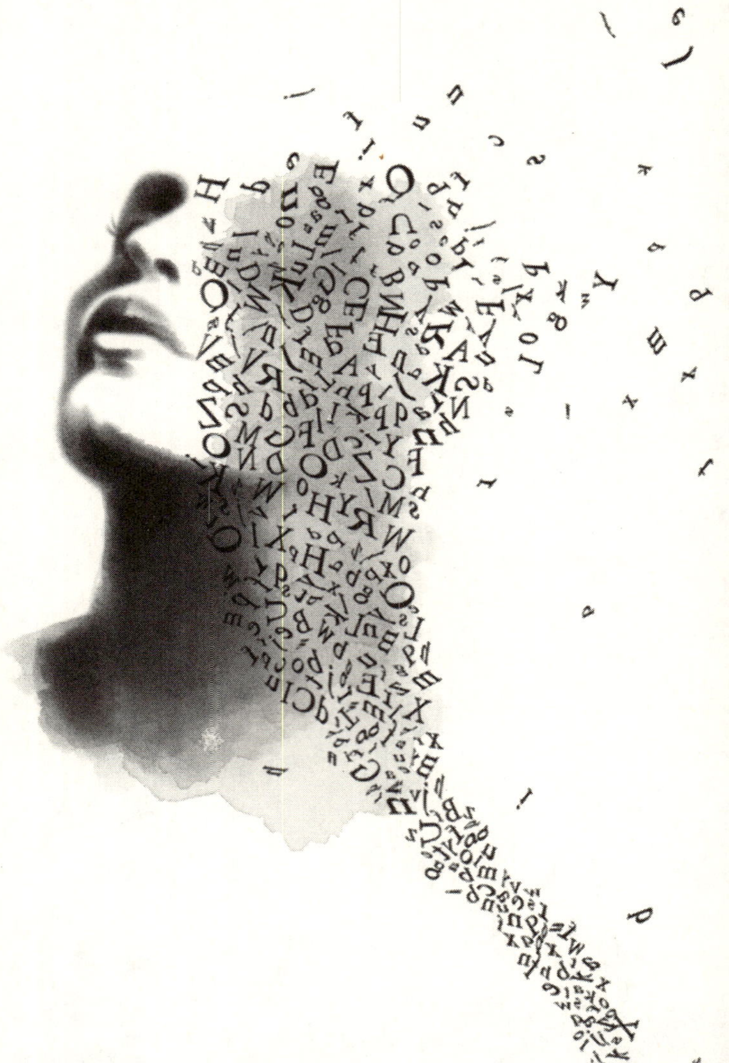

Glee

The way the heart beats wild and free,
The way a thought makes you smile with glee,
This thing that you feel, the magic that you see,
Is not an illusion but as real as You and Me.

The remains of the day

Do I really belong here?
Is my mind truly without fear?
Why do I feel like a hunted deer,
With death not far but clearly near?
But before I go to my flowery bier,
In my mind, it's all too clear,
Love me you never did,
Behind an illusion I just hid.
On the wane now is your sway
Just like the remains of the day.

My little fawn

At the break of dawn
Is born my little fawn,
Scrambling to its feet,
Despite the dust and heat,
Unaware of strife,
Full of a new life.
Its bleats touch my heart,
For us, it's a great new start.
Life in all its forms,
With its seasons and storms,
Has much to offer to us,
And we musn't miss the bus.
Love and peace for all ye go there
To my fawn, dear life forever be fair.

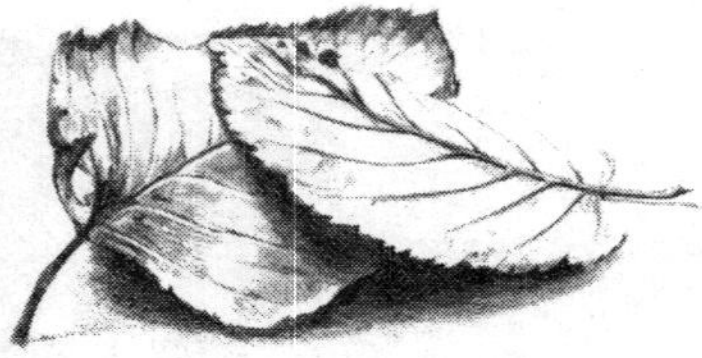